What Do You Like to Do During Spring?

What do you like to do during spring?

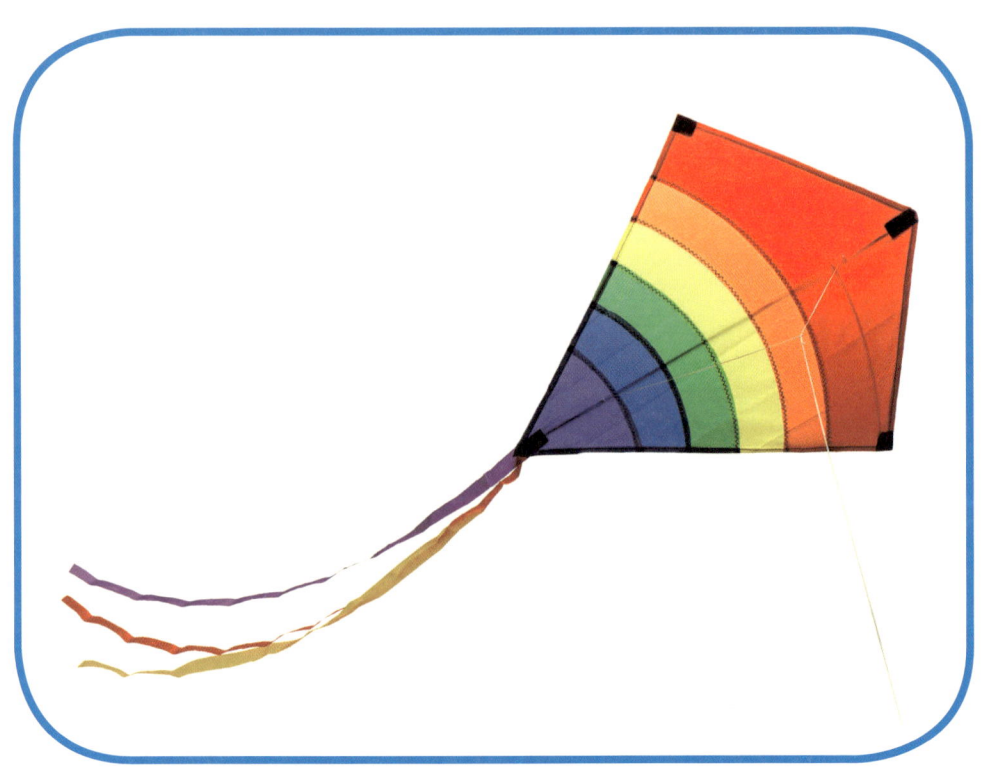

Fly kites.

I like to fly kites
during spring.

What do you like to do during spring?

Feed swans.

I like to feed swans during spring.

What do you like to do during summer?

Build sandcastles.

I like to build sandcastles during summer.

What do you like to do during summer?

Go camping.

I like to go camping during summer.

What do you like to do during fall?

Paint pumpkins.

I like to paint pumpkins during fall.

What do you like to do during winter?

Go sledding.

I like to go sledding during winter.

What do you like to do during winter?

Make snowmen.

I like to make snowmen during winter.

Let's learn more about Thanksgiving Day.

Color the turkey.